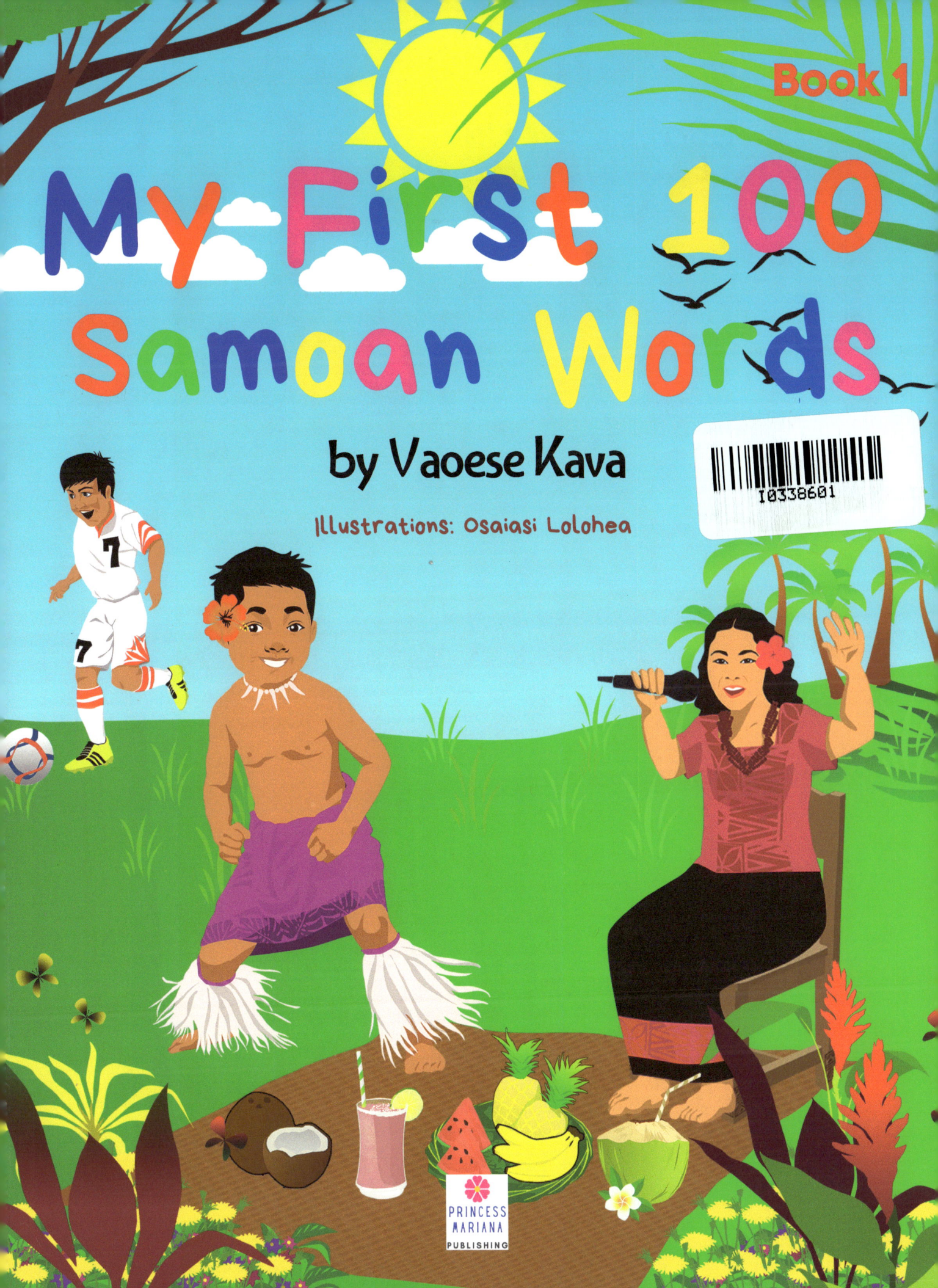

*For My Grandson, Amulek Ualesi
May Your Life Bring Inspiring Stories*

My First 100 Samoan Words - Book 1
(Presented in Basic Phrases in Samoan & English)
Copyright © 2020 by: Princess Mariana Publishers
All rights reserved. No part of this book may be reproduced in any manner whatsoever without written permission of the author and publisher. Except in the case of brief quotations and reviews. Thank you for your support and for buying an authorised edition. For more information, pls.
Contact: #VaoeseLimutauKava :
on Facebook & Instagram
Written By: Vaoese Kava
Illustrations By: Osaiasi Lolohea
ISBN 978-0-6450030-0-0 (hardcover)
ISBN 978-0-6450030-4-8 (paperback)
ISBN 978-0-6450030-1-7 (eBook)
Distributed Worldwide
First Edition Nov. 2020

O lo'u Kasegi (tauusoga) o Ellya 'e fiafia 'e 'Ai

My Cousin Ellya likes to Eat

Oute fiafia 'e Ta'alo ma a'u Uō

I enjoy it when I Play with my Friends

E lelei tele le Pese a Ellya

Ellya can Sing really well

O le matou Fale Samoa lenei

This is our Samoan House

O le matou **Falesa** lea, oute alu ai 'i le **Lotu**

This is our **Chapel**, where I attend **Church**

Sa a'oa'o mai Tamā, oute
Tatalo 'ae oute le'i moe 'i le Po

Father taught me, to Pray
before bedtime at Night

About the Author:

Vaoese Kava "aka" Ese Limutau Noa Aiono has always had a passion for writing since she was a young girl. This later inspired her to complete her Arts and Business Administration studies and earning her MBA from the Australian Institute of Business, South Australia. She's a wife, a mother, and grandmother to the adorable Amulek. Her desire to teach her grandson Samoan led to the completion of this four book series of a Child's first 100+ basic words & phrases in Samoan & English. She hopes that this book series will encourage parents and child to not only learn to speak Samoan but practice fun and healthy family lifestyle habits. Follow her on Instagram & Facebook #VaoeseLimutauKava

PRINCESS MARIANA

PUBLISHING

I Love You

www.ingramcontent.com/pod-product-compliance
Lightning Source LLC
Chambersburg PA
CBHW041155290426
44108CB00002B/73